Bigambul Elder, Uncle Wes Marne AM, is best known
for his storytelling and work as an advocate and
champion for Aboriginal youth and families across
the Greater Sydney Region.

In *Through Old Eyes – Poems by Uncle Wes Marne* we
celebrate with Uncle Wes the 100th anniversary of his
birth, 25 April 1922.

Uncle Wes writes with poignancy, resilience, and
inspiration about our history, our ancestors and of
what he has learnt on his life's journey. His poetry is
an expression of the legacy that he wants to share with
us all. His warmth, connection to culture, and love
for community keeps the fires of Indigenous knowledge
burning bright.

Dr Belinda Russon CEO Tranby Aboriginal Co-operative Limited.

This publication additionally commemorates the
founding of the original BLACKBOOKS by Kevin Cook
in 1982. It demonstrates the commitment of Tranby
Aboriginal Co-operative Limited to strengthen and
share the diverse voices of Aboriginal and Torres Strait
Islander people and communities across Australia.

T0359822

THROUGH
OLD EYES

To the many people, young and old,
who have come into my life
to inspire my poetry.
We have learnt and grown together.
We have disagreed, argued, listened
and learnt from each other.

W.M.

First published 2022 by
BLACKBOOKS®
a division of
Tranby Aboriginal Co-operative Limited.

Reprinted 2022

BLACKBOOKS.online
BLACKBOOKS@tranby.edu.au

A catalogue record for this
book is available from the
National Library of Australia

NATIONAL
LIBRARY
OF AUSTRALIA

ISBN: 978-0-6454282-0-9

Design: Donna Rawlins

Printed in Maryborough, Victoria by McPhersons Printing Group Pty Ltd

PEFC Certified

This product is from
sustainably managed forest
and controlled sources.
Recognised in Australia by
Responsible Wood.

PEFC/21-31-16   www.pefc.org.au

THROUGH OLD EYES

POEMS BY

UNCLE WES MARNE

BLACK
BOOKS

CONTENTS

FOREWORD

A proud Bigambul man, Uncle Wes Marne AM comes from generations of storytellers and knowledge keepers. In this anthology *Through Old Eyes*, Uncle Wes writes with poignancy, resilience, and inspiration about our history, our ancestors, and of what he has learnt on his life's journey. His poetry is an expression of the legacy that he wants to share with us all. His warmth, connection to culture, and love for community keeps the fires of Indigenous knowledge burning bright.

Uncle Wes's collection of poems is for everyone, across all ages, cultures, and denominations. His words invite and enable us all to understand and appreciate the past, serving as a reminder that, in his words, "no one can take our culture from our hands".

This book is the product of a wonderfully creative collaboration between the indomitable Uncle Wes, Tranby – in our 65th year of operations – and our newly re-launched BLACKBOOKS team. Tranby is honored to support Uncle Wes in realising his dream to produce a book of poetry in his 100th year.

Tranby is committed to education as a pathway for our people to attain self-determination and enhance the lives and livelihoods of our Families and our communities. We greatly value the knowledge and learning that our Elders hold – generously share and contribute in supporting our young people and communities. We thank Uncle Wes for trusting Tranby and BLACKBOOKS. We thank and acknowledge all our Elders, past and present, who are the foundation of our being and society as First Nations people.

I am immensely grateful to the BLACKBOOKS and Tranby team, staff and volunteers, for ensuring this book will be the first book published by the newly established BLACKBOOKS. I give special acknowledgement to Debbie Higgison, who has been instrumental in working with Uncle Wes during this process.

In his poetry, Uncle Wes skillfully captures the essence of our land, our people and our past, motivating us to share story, history and preserve knowledge into the future. His words implore us to pay attention to the old ways, to share our reflections and to remember that the spirits are always nearby, walking this journey with us.

Dr Belinda Russon
CEO Tranby Aboriginal Co-operative Limited.

INTRODUCTION

Alicia Talbot (**AT**) *in conversation with Uncle Wes Marne* (**UW**).

AT: I first met Uncle Wes in 2004 when we were introduced to each other by Lily Shearer.

UW: Lily Shearer was the first person who started typing these poems out, that was in the 1990s. In those days I was writing one or two poems a day.

AT: We were all working at Urban Theatre Projects on a new show in Mount Druitt.

UW: Alicia and I got on very well together. Our friendship has lasted. I gave Alicia one of my poetry books and these are many of the same poems that you are about to read.

AT: Uncle Wes is an inspiring artist and storyteller. He is able to share culture, stories and poems to anyone who would like to listen. Uncle Wes often says that when he speaks and writes, his Grandfather is with him. Around the fire, in the room – prompting him in everything. Like so many others I have listened and watched as Uncle Wes shares his poems – at the right time, with the right person, on Country. It seems that these are exactly the words that need to be spoken in that one moment.

UW: These poems are of my life, and I like to share with everybody my life as an Aboriginal man – everything I have done is in these poems.

AT: A direct story of the last 150 years and time immemorial. It is remarkable to listen to and read the words of a storyteller, who shares stories of his grandfather.

UW: These poems are dreams. But I have added a little bit more in here and there – when I say the pig is closing in on me (The Run, page 86) I didn't really run three or four miles, I climbed a tree straight away. But I am not going to say that now. A poem is a story.
A lot of people don't know the Aboriginal way of life and in the early days when we weren't allowed to do this or we weren't allowed to do that, we could speak words.
These words are what has happened.

AT: What made you write these poems in the first place?

UW: Because this was how we lived and behaved in times gone by. The children are not being taught about the old ways, and it is something that they will miss in the future. At the present time and at this stage in my life, I live a lot in the past and these things are all with me all the time.

AT: When I read these poems, I feel content. I can almost hear you speak each word. There is a rhythm to what you say and what you write. Did your grandfather speak like that?

UW: Yes. He was a visionary. He loved talking about the past and what the future held for us. By my grandfather looking into the past and seeing how much had changed in his lifetime, he could visualise what was going to happen in the future. And he wasn't far wrong either.
He is the main reason why I started writing these poems. People like him are with you all the time.

AT: You write a lot about the bush, about Country and you don't seem so keen on the City?

UW: The city has been good to me. It hasn't hurt me. It has made me look at both sides of the different people in this country and I visualise all the time what has happened to our people. I have kept out of trouble, I have lived the Aboriginal cultural life as much as I could in the city. That has helped me to attain the position I am in today. Because there are many people who want to know and understand Aboriginal culture. You don't have to be Aboriginal to want to know about culture. If these poems go into the schools and the children read them it is going to give them something to think about. You can read it for yourself and form your own opinion. And I hope that you can appreciate our old way of life as a way of looking to the future. I hope my children acknowledge and are prepared to follow on.

FEBRUARY 2022

Biographical Notes

BORN 25th April 1922, in 2022 Uncle Wes Marne AM celebrates his 100th birthday.

Uncle Wes Marne is Bigambul man and community elder who has lived and worked on Darug Land in Mt Druitt, Western Sydney for more than four decades. His father's country, Bigambul country, is located in South West Queensland, spanning the Queensland and New South Wales borders and centred on the riverine area between the Macintyre and Weir rivers. His mother's country is Flinders Island.

Uncle Wes's early childhood was one of living in the bush with his extended family where they lived traditionally, as his ancestors had. As a child, he lived tribally on the banks of the river in southern Queensland.

"I still think my happiest times were when I lived on the river in the old tin camp, we didn't have to worry about much at all, we fished and we hunted and we swam."

When he was nine years old, the government walked his family off tribal lands from the Stanthorpe Hills to Deadbird Mission, Ashford northern New South Wales in a journey that took three weeks. Under the control of the government, and the church in some cases, practicing cultural ceremonies, speaking Indigenous language and speaking about their Indigenous heritage was strictly forbidden and punishable by law.

"I never had much education. I never started till I was 10 and I only stayed for one day."

The school he attended had a series of buildings shaped in a horseshoe configuration, but Uncle Wes and his fifteen-or-so Aboriginal classmates weren't allowed in the buildings, instead they were taught in a bough shed – a wall-less structure made of tree branches on the fringe of the school site.

At 11, Wes Marne went wherever he could find work. His first job was carrying water to ring barkers.

"I was a water boy. I used to run around giving everyone a drink of water and it was no easy matter, chasing a lot of men through the bush carrying a hessian water bag about, but anyway it was a living."

He went on to be a boxer, losing most of his teeth in the ring, then there was the "back breaking" work at a tannery, a chicken factory and picking and packaging tobacco all over the country. He also worked as a drover, a miner and served his country in the Korean War.

Uncle Wes and his wife Emma moved to Sydney in the 1960s to give their children a better education. He has outlived four of his children. One baby died from cot death, two were killed in a car crash, another drowned.

Uncle Wes, coming from a long line of storytellers, is committed to sharing the traditional knowledge of his grandfather's creation and dreaming stories, and personal experiences of his life as an Aboriginal man over the last century. He learnt the art of storytelling around the campfire and in the bush listening to his revered grandfather.

"My grandfather told me these stories; my father was a storyteller but his heart wasn't in it. My grandfather carried on the legacy right up until he died. Whenever the stories were told to me as a kid my mother would

question me and say, 'tell me the stories you heard last night'. She wanted to hear the Dreaming stories, the creation stories I was being told, and even though she had heard these stories a hundred times or more she wanted to make sure it was sinking in with me." [1]

"I used to do this years ago [perform the stories for people] but the police had us stopped and, when I was young, Aboriginal people were not allowed to gather in groups to tell or be told their stories. Now that's genocide to stop the culture." [1]

When he arrived in Sydney in the 1960s he was living in Emerton, and was not allowed to tell his stories at schools so he decided to set up in his backyard – he set up a fire bucket and invited families and children from the local Aboriginal community to come join his family to sit around the fire and share his stories. It did not take long for the police to arrive and arrest him for hosting an unlawful gathering – he spent two days in lock-up for sharing his stories. When he was first asked to speak in NSW public schools, the invitation came with a warning: no talk of massacres or genocide or stolen children. "Only Dreaming stories."

Years later his critically acclaimed performance piece "Fire Bucket" at the Sydney Festival and later at the Yirramboi First Nations Arts Festival in Melbourne saw sold out performances with one reviewer commenting, "Uncle Wes, a community elder from Mt Druitt, wove creation stories with personal story, anecdotes and animal wisdom stories moving the listener 'back and forwards across time'. When listening to such a consummate storyteller, colour and sensation can be seen and experienced with vivid and memorable clarity." In his lifetime Uncle Wes has inspired multiple generations through his stories, poetry and performance.

In 2011 Uncle Wes was the proud recipient of the first Nanga Mai Love of Learning Award. The Nanga Mai Awards celebrate and recognise innovation, excellence and achievement in Aboriginal education in NSW public schools, school communities and the Department of Education and Training offices. In 2012 he received the Western Sydney University Community Award in acknowledgement of his Aboriginal culture and education work.

Uncle Wes is a member of the Mount Druitt and Districts Reconciliation Group which, for the past 22 years, has organised a reconciliation walk in Mt Druitt. This program has continued to grow due to the committed and dedicated work of Uncle Wes and his fellow committee members. Uncle Wes dedicates his life to helping our children and men who have been incarcerated to get their lives back on track by helping them to regain confidence to advocate on their own behalf. He works as an advocate for his people at Centrelink, the Department of Housing, Community Services, Juvenile Justice and he is a regular visitor to young Aboriginal men in prison and detention.

Uncle Wes, along with many of his peers and friends in the Mt Druitt and Districts Reconciliation Group, support Aboriginal self-determination and advocate for equal rights and respect for Australia's First Peoples across all areas. They are also committed to helping non-Indigenous people to understand our true history.

In June 2022 Uncle Wes Marne was awarded an AM in the Australian Queen's Birthday Honours for his significant service to the Indigenous community of Western Sydney.

---

[1] https://www.buzzfeed.com/allanclarke/this-indigenous-man-is-trying-to-save-a-dying-tradition

CAMPFIRE DREAMING

Coal Dreaming

He sat alone cross legged
And looked into his fire of dreams
No matter what he thought he could see
In it there, it seemed.
He could see himself as a young boy
In the coals he could see himself grow
Into a hunter to be proud of
Into a warrior that all would know.

His wife and children were there too
He could see them as plain as day
He didn't need the fire to remember them
They were never far away.
He could see his relations and people
The ones that he'd watched fade away
One at a time they had all gone on
The last had moved on today.

To watch over this land is his duty
He feels all alone it seems
But he knows he can always have company
There is always his campfire of dreams.

THE MAKER

Listen to the stories
That come from round the fire
Listen and take notice
For the spirits are nearby.

They listen to hear what I tell you
If the stories that I tell you are right
The stories must forever be told
So listen carefully, to me tonight.

The stories passed down through the Dreaming
From the Maker of every thing
Who made the hills and mountains
The plains, rivers and springs.

Every single thing that he made
Was made for you to use
But use them well and use them right
They must not be abused.

Everything has a purpose
The animals, the trees, each thing
Even the mighty eagle
That soars on gigantic wings.

The insects and the rodents
All have their tiny part
He made them for a purpose
He made them from the heart

He gave us all these natural things
So that we can live and thrive
So watch over them also
Or nothing will survive.

So listen and remember my stories
For what I have told you is right
Many more stories will come to you
But remember this one tonight.

Campfire Dreaming

The fire was banked
Billy on the side
He stretched out on his blanket
He was ready for the night.

He liked this time of evening
When everything was at rest
Only the night animals stirring
The bush was at its best.

The evening breeze was moving
Rustling the trees above
Contentment wrapped around him
And he gazed at the stars above.

Tonight they seemed to be brighter
They all seemed bigger somehow
And stories came rushing back to him
As he tried to remember them now.

Each light up there was a campfire
Lit by a warrior of old
The brighter the light, the better the man
Who has travelled on before.

Did his father and *his* father before him
Stoke their own glowing campfires bright?
Did they sit around them talking
Of the good times every night?

There is a dark spot in the middle
Where he couldn't see a light
That is where he was going!
When it came time for his fire to light.

MY PLACE

My Prayer

Oh Spirit of the Dreamtime
Look down on us now
You guided our forefathers
Your wisdom is needed now.

We have wandered from the old ways
Your help is what we lack
Don't turn your face away from us
We want your wisdom back.

Help us to turn around
Take us back to the past
Take us back to the Dreamtime
Let us make a new start

To times of hunting and fishing
When our lives were on the land
To times of peace and contentment
When time was in our hands.

Two hundred years you have been away
We have turned our backs on you
Reach out your hand and help us now
To go back to the ways we knew.

PEACE

To walk through the scrub and up the hill
To lie on my back to take my fill
Of the sky and the clouds as they hurriedly race
To far off horizons away from this place.

I think of the times when I was a lad
Of fires and stories that made my heart glad
Tales of the Dreaming of rivers and hills
The tales of the Serpent are with me still.

Who made the trees, the animals and streams,
The people and stars that forever gleam?
They were there in the stories that were always sung
Around the fires when I was young.

I often think of those wonderful days
When we were one with the land and one with its ways
When the sky was our cover and the ground was our bed
We followed the old ones wherever they led.

We came from the land, from our Mother Earth
To stay in this country, the land of our birth
To lie here in peace as the times roll on
Ten thousands of years have already gone.

To be here at dawn as the land unfolds

To be here at night when the darkness rolls

To be here when I'm young, to be here when I'm old

Just to be here keeps me enthralled.

RETURN

Go on ahead and leave me here
I'll stop a while to rest
I'll catch up to you later on
Before the sun has set.

This is my father's country
And his father walked this land
I feel their presence near me
I know they are close at hand.

They must have hunted this river
In the times of long ago
This is where they lit their fires
And camped when the sun was low.

I wonder what they want of me
Why they are calling me near
Are they trying to tell me something?
Something for just my ears.

Are they glad that I have come here?
Or have I failed them in some way?
They might wonder how long I've been here
And if I've come to stay.

So I'll be along about sundown
By then they will let me know
If they're happy with me being here
Or if they'd rather that I go.

DAY

The sky starts to lighten
As the day comes alive
There is magic here
In the movement of life.

As the dark night wanes
And the day comes alive
The birds are awake
The bees in their hives.

The land rings out with the noises they make
The kingfisher's laugh is filling the light
The bellbirds and magpies warble and wake
Tongues by the thousands in the fading of night.

To greet the sun and farewell the dark
Each creature out looking to feast
Wings gently stretched and feet on the move
The light glowing in the east.

Let us soar up here on the morning's breeze
And follow the current wherever it leads
Or go to the north where the brolgas dance
To the west, in that great expanse.

The roo and the emu are on the feed
The dingo hunts with a hungry need
Everything is now at daylight best
Then in the heat soon all will rest.

A Puzzle

How long have they lived here?
Where did they come from to here?
There are hundreds of different stories
But only one I want to hear.

I wonder if it's true they walked
Over that long forgotten bridge
Had they followed the food before them
And found this place to live?

Or did everything start right here
And go from here to there?
And put to rest the stories
That they came from there to here.

GNARLED FRIEND

A huge colossus standing there
Its arms stretched to the sky
A thousand years of growing
It's seen what's passed it by.

Could it tell of ancient people
Who've sat beneath for rest?
Would it tell of little children
Who had climbed up to its crest?

How many birds have nested
In its strong and ancient arms?
How many birds have sung their songs
Of the bush and all its charms?

How it has suffered the elements
As the seasons passed it by
All standing at attention
Its canopy in the sky.

How it stretches its arms in the morning
Reaching them out to the sun
And then along about evening
Bows them down for the day is done.

Easy Life

Could I go back to the old ways
Back to living off the land
Back to the hunt and the wild, wild bush
Living off what is at hand?

Could I take up the woomera and spear
And make my gunyah of brambles and bark
And use the killer boomerang
And sleep whenever it gets dark?

Oh could I make this transition
Could I make this change
Could I go out and live there
And over the country range?

Or will I stay here
With the things I would miss
Like coffee and sugar and salt and tea
And my children's loving kiss?

My Land

A thousand years it would take to show
Ten thousand more to learn and know
What makes this land so great and fine
What makes me proud when I say, "It's mine".

It's watched over my people for thousands of years
Guided them through their triumphs and tears
Their dances and stories come from the land
It gave shelter and food to those nomadic bands.

But most of all it has given us peace –
And this will go on until all time has ceased
For this land is ours – it's not only mine
This wonderful place – so great and so fine.

My Place

Come with me and let's behold
The wonders as this land unfolds
Let's be up there before the dawn
And see the beauty as the day is born.

Look back behind. Look! We can see
The land as it stretches out to the sea
The beaches that stretch and the islands small
To the south, and north, we can see tham all.

And there is the looming mountain crest
That guards the slopes that roll in from the west
The rugged peaks like sentinels old
Appears as the morning mists unroll.

Across the gulf to the far Top End
Across its domain to the north land's end
Then south where the Kimberley Ranges go
Then east to the desert where salt bushes grow.

This land stretches far as the eye can see
And it waits out there for you and me
Its harshness and beauty are all as one
My place that I love in the shimmering sun.

INDIGENOUS ONES

TEACHER

He walks proud and tall in my dreams
When I'm awake he is with me, it seems
When the sound of the bush is beckoning me on
It's his voice in the breeze that calls me along.

I think of the times when he held my hand
When he showed and taught me the way of the land
What not to touch and what not to eat
His voice and his actions guiding my feet.

The birds and the animals, he knew them all
The prints on the ground and the trees so tall
To hunt and to gather what we need
To share what we have and never know greed.

Indigenous Ones

Indigenous people from this earth's lands
Now is the time for us all to join hands
To let the world know we are still here
Let's do it now – for this is our year.

Let the world know that our culture's alive
Let the world know that we have survived
Let them all know that we are still strong
Let them all know that we are not wrong.

While there is one to tell stories
And there is one to hear
While we still sing our songs
They will know we are still here.

While we still do our dances
And still hunt our lands
No one can take
Our culture from our hands.

Let the old ones tell the stories
Let the young ones hear and learn
Tell them of our days of glory
So that for more they will yearn.

And they will tell their young ones
And teach them what we were told
And we will be here forever
And our culture will never grow old.

MOTHER EARTH

He is the ultimate hunter
A bushman without peer
Nothing is safe when he is hunting
With his ancient woomera and spear.

But what of the one who goes with him
The one who walks in his tracks
Usually with one child behind her
And another on her back.

With a coolamon under her arm
A dilly bag around her waist
She wanders along gathering
Food in an everlasting chase.

She wanders back and forth
Gathering the seed for bread
Looking and digging for yams
To be cooked in the camp ahead.

At dusk she builds their shelter
And prepares the evening food
Always busy moving around
There is always something to do.

Next time you look at a picture
Of a warrior of the land
Look for the one behind him
For the one who is always on hand.

She is the eternal companion
The one you rarely see
And she is the reason that life goes on
Her and the children at her knee.

Grandfather

His face was strong but gentle
His voice was smooth and clear
His hands were big and supple
His eyes were brown and clear.

He was old and bent when I knew him
His race was nearly run
He liked to sit and tell me
Of the days when he was young.

He always smiled to greet me
Always had a kind word to say
He always had something to tell me
To help me on my way.

He liked the warmth of the summer
But when the winter winds blew
He'd pull his blanket around him
As the warmth of his fire grew.

Then the time came when he left us
His Spirit went in the night
His weary body could take no more
He had lost the long last fight.

I still think of him as special

And as the seasons go and come

I know that he is happy

In his place in the warmth of the sun!

MOTHER'S LOVE

I was standing outside this local pub
When someone touched my arm
And a voice asked could I help her
And she said she meant no harm.

This dark skinned lady stood there
On her face was a look of pain
And the sadness in her deep brown eyes
I never want to see again.

She asked if I was going to the city
I said I was heading there
The tears rolled down like raindrops
Her face was lined with care.

She said she had a daughter
Who the government had taken away
And this mother was still waiting
For her daughter to come home to stay.

She was two years old when they took her
They said it was for the best
But did they have some God-given right
To take her from the breast?

All these years she had waited
But there was no sign or word
It was as if her daughter had just disappeared
From the very face of the world.

She said that if I should see her
Tell her that her mum was alone
Tell her that she was waiting here
That she would always be here at home.

And if and when I saw her
Tell her not to wait
Tell her please to hurry
So she did not come too late.

LORE

He walked away at sun up
His step was long and strong
He waved his hand in a gesture
It meant "come follow on".

He lifted his eyes to the mountains
Then upwards to the sky
He looked for clouds in the distance
To see if a storm was high.

He strolled as I ran beside him
He smiled with his hand on my head
"Whatever you get from this place,
Only take whatever you need.

Whatever you take from this beautiful place
Remember you have to earn."
I listened hard to what he said
and tried my best to learn.

He stopped and pointed to places –
To places I shouldn't go
He led me along the pathways
And told me what I should know.

He turned around at sundown
He said, "Now we're going home
Remember what I've told and showed you
One day you'll be on your own."

THE HUNTER

He trails along behind
Toes kicking up the dust
His little feet are aching
But to keep up is a must.

His mother is ahead of him
His father's on the wing
His mind's alert and racing
He dreams of his favourite things.

He is out there with his father
Spear and club in his growing hands
Together they are fearless
They are the kings of their rugged land.

No tracks will escape their glances
They notice every mark
Everything is a map to him
Like the paintings on the bark.

The kangaroo leaps fast away
And they take up on the chase
With these two great hunters after him
He is just not in the race.

And when the rest of the hungry clan
Say their hunt has brought them nil
He will stroll in nonchalantly
And present them with his kill.

And forever they will sing their songs
And tell stories of his skill
How he never went out hunting
Without bringing home a kill.

TEMPTATION

Stay and listen to me, lad
Don't you go away
The city is no place for us
And it's so far away.

Your mother wants you here at home
And I am on her side
For I have seen the city too
And it's enough to make you cry.

Especially if you were born out here
This is the place for you
You've been listening to others talk
The city is no place for you.

Stay with me and I'll teach you
My knowledge while you grow
About the bush and the animals there
That Kooris all should know.

To hunt and track as I was taught
When we were a tribal band
When we were lords of all we sought
When this was our un-stolen land.

I'll tell you of the Dreaming
And the maker of everything here
I'll teach the songs and the dances
That tell how and why we are here.

We'll hunt roo and turkey together
And we'll make the emu run
We'll leave here and head out on walkabout
Way out on the western run.

So stay with us, son, at home here
We'll fish and hunt for our needs
Don't go away to the city
That place full of hatred and greed.

LOST

To walk into the clearing
Was the hardest thing to do
Mum was talking with her father
The words were reaching through.
The horse and cart were loaded
I looked around and said,
"I can't go with you now, Mum
I'm gonna wait for Dad."
"Come on son it's getting late.
It's time for us to go!"
I looked around the clearing
Our possessions were so few
I didn't want to leave
The only home I ever knew.
"Come on now, get in the cart
Stop acting like a fool!
We're moving closer into town
It's time to go to school."

Why?

I watched him walk away that time
When he went off to war
I felt so lost and lonely
As I had never felt before.

"You're the man now that I'm going
Look after Mum for me
Remember the things I've taught you
Stay out here where you are free.

I didn't know why he was going
Why couldn't I go along?
We had always been together
The urge to follow was strong.

I felt her arms around me
In our sorrow we entwined
My body was numb with sorrow
Her tears were mixed with mine.

I'll never forget that parting.
I was only five years old.

Forlorn

We waited at the station
The train was nearly due
Our hearts beating like a tomtom
Our wishes coming true.

We were waiting there to meet him
At last he was coming home
Three and a half years of waiting
I wanted to see him alone.

I wanted to tell him my secrets
For him to come back and say
We're going back to the mountains
We are going back there to stay.

The train pulled in beside us
The policemen held us back
I strained my eyes to see him
The soldiers had come back.

When the crowd had thinned we waited still
Just for a glimpse of him
But he wasn't there when the crowd had gone
What had become of him?

Happiness Is

Happiness to me is two children playing
Their faces alight with joy
Happiness is two children laughing
A little girl, a little boy.

Contentment is two children walking
Their hands trusting in my care
Contentment is two children talking
When their secrets they with me share.

Happiness is two children smiling
Brown eyes aglow with joy
Dark curly hair always shining
A little girl, a little boy.

Contentment is two children listening
To the stories that we share
Contentment is answering their questions
For my knowledge is beyond compare.

Happiness is two children sharing
Each other's company with joy
Happiness is two children caring
A little girl, a little boy.

The Bunyip

Time for sleep my babies
Lie there and be very quiet
The Bunyip is out hunting
And he only hunts at night.

He is looking for his supper
So don't you make a noise
He is looking for something nice to eat
And he just loves little girls and boys.

You know the tales of what he does
To children who won't go to sleep
So make sure your eyes are closed up tight
And I'll lie here at your feet.

He'll be gone in the morning when you awake
For he does not like the light
He goes and hides in the deepest scrub
Just waiting for the night.

So go to sleep my babies
The Bunyip's out tonight
He is looking for the little ones
Whose eyes are not closed tight!

EMMA

Little brown-skinned girl
Of the Dreaming lands
Eyes full of love
Always near at hand.

I have watched you grow
From your very first day
Your laugh and your smile
Makes my every day.

If you were playing
And if you fell
You'd run to me
To kiss it well.

I love you when you're sleeping
When you jump, and skip and hop
But most of all I love you
When you say, "I love you Pop".

THE ROAD

THE ROAD

When he first started wandering
There was so much he should know
And he wasn't at all prepared for
The hard road he'd have to hoe.

Born on his Country not black and not white
He wandered the roads to the left and the right
There was no one to help him, no one to show
But he started to learn of that hard road to hoe.

And no matter what job he went for
He was always the last they put on
And was always first the boss would let go
On that hard road he was learning to hoe.

From the fruit in the south to the cane in the north
Wherever he went, how far he went forth
Cross country he travelled, he went to and fro
It was always that hard road to hoe.

But times change by and by – it's much easier now
For his young family starting to grow
And he hopes that for them in the future they plan
They've an easier road to hoe.

DEPENDABLE

The old man walked to the bustling home yard
A worried look upon his face
He had expected him this morning
But he couldn't see a trace.

The horses were saddled and ready
The packhorses loaded with gear
The young men eager to be moving
The old man still kept them near.

He had told them of the country
That they were headed for
He'd been out there himself sometimes
Many years before.

The men that he had gone with
Were Bushmen first and last
One bad mistake made out there
Could be their very last.

A noise behind spun him around
And away went the look of fear
"Of course I knew you'd come old friend
If you knew I needed you here.

"You have not changed a bit old mate
Aside from the grey in your hair
But your loving black face has warmed my dreams
I could cry because you are here.

"I won't offer you the use of a gun
For you have your woomera and spear
And there's no need for anything else
For you to survive out here.

"My sons are young and headstrong
They think they know this land
But I've stressed to them what I know is true
You're the leader of this band."

The tall dark man stood steady
He stood straight and proud
He would have been noticed anywhere
Standing out in any crowd.

The young men were now mounted
Keen to be on the track
The dark man turned to his old loyal friend
"We'll go now – but I'll bring them back."

HOOKED

I saw him yesterday morning
And vowed that he'd be mine
I'd have him in the coals that night
As sure as the sun will shine.

I'd never felt so keen before
As I made this hungry wish
I would do anything to have him
Today I must have that fish.

I searched around for an hour or more
Till I found beneath a log
Just the bait that I was looking for
In the dirt – a little black frog.

I soon had him in the water
There was no time to waste
My imagination was running wild
And that fish I sure could taste.

I sat there still for hours
Holding onto that empty line
While under the bank on the other side
I saw two fish eyes shine.

But I went to bed so hungry
For my tucker bag was bare
I'll try again tomorrow
For I know he'll still be there.

I dreamt I could hear him laughing
And poking fun at me
He said I was his prisoner
While he was swimming free.

I thought over what he'd told me
And I knew that he was right
I couldn't stay forever
And my hunger was a blight.

So I rolled my swag this morning
And started on my way
Lying to myself and saying
He was too old and tough anyway.

Toy

A half-bred border collie
I found him on one night
Up in the New England ranges
Half dead, a sorry sight.

I took him home and fed him
And that was the very start
Of an extra special friendship
From then we were never apart.

We went everywhere together
To towns and to bush jobs
And everyone that met me knew
The rule "No dog – no job".

And on one dangerous morning
A snake was ready to strike
In a flash old Toy had caught him
Broke his back with his loyal bite.

I would lay out a hundred hidden traps
He would soon find every one
In winter when the times were hard
In any weather on the midnight run.

No matter what I was doing
He was never far away
He was always there behind me
No matter what time of day.

He was poisoned with ten eighty
I found him in the yard
I didn't know how much I'd miss him
I never thought I'd take it so hard.

I will never forget that faithful dog
He was the best mate I ever had
Toy will always be a part of me
When I think of the good times we had.

Bushmen

Getting old, stiff and battered
His joints are all on fire
Finding it harder to move around
Until the sun has stoked its fire.

When the warmth of the sun is on him
His body loosens up
His blood starts running more quickly
For he is no more a pup.

There's a trap in the river to be looked at
There might be a fish there today
For the river is running a bit dirty
So the fish should be moving this way.

Then he'll go for a walk to the corner store
And if the time is right
He might catch old Tom on that corner
And they'll go for a beer and a skite.

In the old days they were drovers together
Pushed cattle right through the drought
Their memories were still young and lively
Though Father Time had dealt them a bout.

They had driven the cattle through desert
Crossed all the wild rivers in flood
Rode the roughest of galloping outlaws
When the job still fueled their young blood.

They'd relive all the times and the places
When they rode all over the land
Of the horses, the men and the faces
And friends made with the shake of a hand.

SCARED

Cold and wet and dreary
The rain kept tumbling down
Huddled against the trunk of a tree
He surely felt half drowned.

He had built a mound of sticks
On which to stand upon
To keep his feet out of the mud
But the feeling in them was gone.

He thought of the day before
When he'd been told to move along
"Get out of town and don't come back
You are not wanted here. Get gone."

It didn't matter that he'd worked
Around the town for weeks
He'd have been all right if he'd stayed at home
But he'd walked upon their streets.

He'd been shown the way out of the town
And told to not come back
"We don't want your kind hanging round.
We're sorry – but you're black."

His heart ached deep inside him
And he shifted on his swag
He hadn't known that being black
Would make his shoulders sag.

The anger welled inside him
As he wondered what to do
What had he done to warrant this?
Born black – that's it – he knew.

THE PUG

I was working in western Queensland
On a railway relaying gang
There were over sixty workers
There was never a tougher clan.

Most were easy to get on with
A few didn't like us blacks
I fought one of them one evening
And laid him on his back.

I thought I was Joe Louis
I thought I was the best
But four fights and five weeks later
All I wanted to do was rest.

Even though I was the victor
I was feeling sick and sore
I was sorry the fight had started
It was getting to be all out war.

One Sunday while relaxing
Trying to get some rest
The noise from the bottom camp
Disturbed me in my quest.

They had with them this fighter
He was supposed to be the best
He had beat everyone before him
He was Champion of the West.

I was sick of all this fighting
It was really getting me down
To beat him wasn't the answer
There was always another round.

I went down the first time he hit me
The punch wouldn't have dented my hat
I lay there while they counted
I thought finally that is that.

I remembered it years later
I still wasn't quite at rest
I wonder if I had stood up to him
Would I have been Champion of the West?

A Visit

I caught the train this morning
I'm going to visit some mates
I know that I'll be welcome
Away from the city's haste.

I know they'll be glad to see me
They've asked me a dozen times
To go out there to visit them
I can roll up any old time.

They came down here once to visit
But they didn't stay for long
Only a week was too much for them
They packed up and they were gone.

So I'm going out to stay with them
I'm going to hunt and fish
I'm stuff myself with tasty wild game
For this is what I have missed.

I might build myself an old tin hut
Down on the river bend
And find the life I used to lead
Out here with my life-long friends.

I'll get rid of the stink of the city
Fill my lungs with fresh clean air
Out here where things are not gritty
Out here with my friends to share.

THE RUN

I was hot and tired from walking
My swag felt like it weighed a ton
So I was looking for some cooling shade
Any place in out of the sun.

Then I found this shady bushy tree
A hundred yards off to the side of the road
It was just the place I wanted
So I prepared to drop my load.

A grunt and a snort behind me
Quickly made me spin around
And there was this huge boar charging
He was burning across the ground.

So I started desperately running
My feet reaching for more ground
The pig was right behind me
And making some horrible sounds!

I hit the main road flying
I still had my billy and swag
Those things to me were precious
I was clutching them real bad.

That boar he couldn't gain on me
No matter how he strived
For when I reached the open road
I went into overdrive.

I knew I had to reach a town
Before I ran out of breath
I knew I couldn't falter
To hesitate meant death.

When I finally reached a little town
With my boots torn from my feet
I fell and kissed the dusty dirt
In the middle of the street.

So all you Olympic runners
If you want to make it big
I'll take you out into the dusty scrub
And I'll train you with that pig.

Wander Lust

At times I've felt so lonely
And times I've felt so bad
Alone amongst a thousand people
Sometimes I've felt so sad.

I've walked and worked this country
For more than twenty years
Never worried, about anything
But now I've come to here.

I've done the things I've wanted to
Been to places I wanted to see
But when I think back I was running away
From the things that meant most to me.

I always thought I wanted the thrill
To keep moving and see what was over the hill
Just to be out on the road and gone
To reach the next town – and then move on.

There were that places I could have stayed
Then found excuses to be on my way
Another job – another place
Keep on moving as if life was a race.

So what have I got for all those years
Of following the sun? Just nagging fears
My legs are tired, my body is worn
But I know as always I'll move on at dawn.

Which Way?

His dreams last night had been troubled
He had tossed and turned all night
He had tried to put it behind him
He put his head down and cried.

He had dreamed again of his people
They had been on his mind for days
He kept drinking to forget them
But the thoughts wouldn't go away.

This wasn't the place he belonged
His home was not in the city
He bowed his head and covered his face
He was filled with despair and self pity.

A hundred times he'd told himself
To leave and go away
But he kept putting it off till tomorrow
For tomorrow was another day.

He would be out of here in the morning
He said as he got to his feet
But just one more drink to straighten up
Then he headed for the street.

CAGED

I look to the tips of the mountains
As the sun behind them sets
Just looking makes me lonely
I would like to go home again.

I sit in this yard and its bareness
Behind these high stone walls
I look at these men here with me
They seem to not worry at all.

But tonight I'll be free again
And again I'll be able to go
To the land that stretches before me
To the places that I know.

And the trees bend down before me
And the stream makes its winding way
Down the gullies that slope around me
In my home at the closing of day.

When I'm out I vow I'll never
Do the things that put me here
I'll go back to the ones who love me
A thousand miles from here.

The Let Down

Ten years of dreaming
Of walking that track
After all those long years
At last coming back.
Around the next bend
Then up the last hill
Left at the old gum tree
That grows there still.

He broke through the bush
To the clear open space
Disappointment was bitter
This wasn't his place.
This was not what he'd yearned for
There was nothing he knew
Just one wall of a shack was still standing
The bush had claimed its due.

PAYMENT TO COME

DEVASTATED

I'm standing out here in the outland
Watching the sun as it sets
Surely there is no more wonderful sight
Than the sun as it goes to rest.

The old days must have been wonderful
Before the white man set his feet
And did his best to ruin this land
And his best was enough to succeed.

First he came with the convict labour
Then he came with the horse and axe
No thought of conservation
That wasn't in their acts.

Push, ring bark and poison
Was all those white men knew
With not a thought of the future
They did what they came here to do.

You ask do we still want our homeland
Do we want it back at all?
After it has been destroyed
Now is it worth much at all?

Invasion Day

"Lie there quiet my brother
I have never seen this before
A while ago there was nothing
Now look what is on the shore!"

    "Have you ever seen such a big canoe
    And the small ones that came from it
    And the men that have landed there on the shore
    And the beach – do they think they own it?"

"I have never seen such as these
And their bodies are not bare.
And their skin is the colour of pale white clay
Look at the clothes they wear!"

    "The sticks that they carry in their hands
    They make an awful noise
    Smoke and fire explodes from them
    I think they are weapons of war."

"Let us go back to the rest of the clan
And tell of this troubling sight
Maybe these men will be gone in the morning
Maybe they're just staying the night."

"The Elders will know what should be done
But I have never known such fear
I don't want to face their weapons
I think they are stronger than spears"

"I hope they'll be gone tomorrow."

"Maybe they will go away..."

*How little did they know they'd seen
The first Invasion Day.*

Dream On

We are strangers in our own country
Though we've lived here for thousands of years
Any trials we met we mastered
And the land held for us no fears.

Everything was as it should be
The land gave us food and rest
And we wandered the land as we wanted
This was the life we loved best.

But two hundred years of suppression
Two hundred years of strife
Have left us with just dregs of dignity
They have taken all but our lives.

What is a life without honour?
What's life without being free?
There isn't much to look forward to
For the likes of you and me.

We've now lost so much of our culture
Our Dreaming stories near gone
Our dancing and singing near over
The Old Ones are left all alone.

The new generation is lagging
Not much of the old ways stand
Forgotten are the ways of their people
Forgotten are the ways of the land.

Can we start again all over
With our youngest children first?
Teach them right from the cradle
While for knowledge and wisdom they thirst.

Our land and our people were happy
We were all taught right from wrong
Let us start right from the beginning
And one day again soon we'll be strong.

Lost Values

My heart and mind are troubled
My courage is wearing thin
I look at my people around me
I don't know where to begin.

Greed's high on the list with jealousy
The fight for power is all around
So many are out to break you
No matter where you are found.

JUDGE

People of the past can you see
This land that you once roamed free?

Do you like the change in this country of yours
The loss of the culture that for eons endured?

The thrill of the hunt has nearly gone
The dances are few and so are the songs.

Not much respect for the old ones now
And greed is rife and money is power.

You had what you carried without wanting for more
And your life was secure made so by your laws

So ones of the past do you turn away
From what you have seen of your people today?

DOWN BUT NOT OUT

As young men we couldn't see
The edge of our tribal lands
Now a few yards of dirt, a little tin hut
The rest stolen from our hands.

Once we roamed all over this land
Hunting for things to eat
All that we can see now
Are miles of shimmering wheat.

The animals no longer
Come down to feed and drink
The fish are floating belly up
The rivers are one big stink.

The trees with their ancient tribal marks
Have long been all cut down
The sacred places have been destroyed
Bora grounds are under the plough.

We need to stand up and be counted
Let our voices be clearly heard
Let them know this land is rightfully ours
It is not just any piece of dirt.

We don't need a flag to know it
We have known for thousands of years
And if we should die tomorrow
Let us be buried on our land out here.

They have tried to take our culture
To destroy us in this way
So teach the children our stories and songs
In them we'll have our say.

And in time we will be counted
In time we will be back
We will look again on our land with pride
Mother Earth again be back.

Payment to Come

From England came the invaders
To a country that was not theirs
They killed and took what they wanted
And nothing they met with was spared.

They came and took what they wanted
With lies and cheating and guns
Whole bands of people were slaughtered
As though it was sport and was fun.

They took the women and used them
And killed the men out of hand
The atrocities they committed
Against the originals of this land.

What sort of people were they?
A conscience is what they lacked
To deliberately try to commit genocide
Because the natives' skins were black.

Do they truly believe their religion?
They said we must learn of the Lord
And follow the ways that He taught us
But He did not approve of the sword.

When the time comes to meet with our maker
Whether it is our Spirit or whether it's theirs
Who will be asked to make payment
And who will be found in arrears?

WORRIED

I fear losing the ways of my people now
That if I do, I'll be lost somehow
The future looks dark, I can't see the light
As I ask myself what is right.

If I tell my children of the olden days
Is it a waste of time, if it's not their ways?
Their time is now – not in the past
My ways feel near gone, but can they last?

Stony Ground

The year of Indigenous People
Has now drawn to an end.

Is our road ahead now straight
Or does it still have bumps and bends?

Have we finally been accepted?
Does our future look more sound?

Do we move on to greener pastures
Or are we still on stony ground?

Acknowledgements

I would like to acknowledge and thank all the people who
have supported me over the years, especially:

My late wife Emma; my daughters Melanie Marne and Louise
Marne; Ian John Dixon; my grandchildren and great-grandchildren,
nieces and nephews; Aunty Jenny Ebsworth and the Ebsworth
Family; Aunty Edna, Uncle Alan, and the Watson family;
Debbie Higgison her family and parents, Pam and Colin;
Uncle Greg Simms; Uncle Danny Eastwood; Jamie Eastwood;
Lily Shearer; Alicia Talbot; Rosie Dennis; Lyn Leerson and
the Mt Druitt and Districts Reconciliation Committee;
Baabayn Aboriginal Corporation; Kallico Catering – Nene
and Daryll Brown; Joyce Dukes; Father Paul Hanna;
Father Pat Mullins; Ed Husic MP, Member for Chifley; Roger
Price, former Member for Chifley; Stephen Bali, Member for
Blacktown; Tony Bleasdale, Mayor of Blacktown; Staff at Blacktown
Arts Centre; Staff at Carriageworks; Solid Ground Artists in
Residence Program; 2020 Solid Ground Artists in Residence,
Monks (Shannon Smith) and IZZY (Jake Ballard); Chifley College
Dunheved Campus; Graceades Cottage; Patricia Formosa;
Ivanka Pelikan; Brad and Jennell Burrows; Karen Issacs and
Oak Hill College; Dub Leffler; Jamie James; Patrice Wills;
my late friends Coral McLean and Ann McPherson.

The cover and internal images in this book were photographed in various
locations including Blacktown, Tingha and Dead Bird Mission, and are all
© Jamie James. "Always made on Country, in collaboration with Uncle Wes."
JAMIE JAMES www.jamesphoto.com.au

This publication marks the start of a collaboration between BLACKBOOKS® a division of Tranby Aboriginal Co-operative Limited and Running Water Community Press.

BLACKBOOKS® is working to establish itself across the Australian (Global) literary and publishing supply chain through a series of strategic interventions aimed at creating an eco-system of authority and expertise led by Aboriginal and Torres Strait Islander Elders, content creators, cultural producers and community led development organisations.

For more information about our work please contact:
www.BLACKBOOKS.online
BLACKBOOKS@tranby.edu.au

Running Water Community Press is a community-controlled publisher in Mparntwe Alice Springs that is run by and for its authors. It is the only independent press in the Northern Territory and is committed to First Nations truth-telling and storytelling from remote areas.

For more information about our work please contact:
www.runningwatercommunitypress.com
contact@runningwatercommunitypress.com